LOVE
AWAKENS
YOU

LOVE AWAKENS YOU

A Surprisingly Refreshing Guide
on Reconnecting with Peace,
Happiness and Self-Confidence

CINDI BUCKLEY

ISBN: 979-8-88759-243-5 (paperback)
ISBN: 979-8-88759-244-2 (ebook)

Contents

1. Introduction   ix

2. Definitions   xi

3. History   xiii

4. How to use this Book   xvii

5. Section 1 – Inspirational Sayings   1

6. Section 2 – 4-Line Verses   27

7. Section 3 – Answers   41

   Home   43

   Independence   45

   Individuality   47

   Comparison   49

   Competition   51

   Conflict   53

   Judgement   55

   Denial   57

   Anger   59

Pain	61
Doubt	63
Fear	65
Ego	67
Control	69
Duality	71
Death	73
Enemies	75
Specialness	77
Responsibility	79
Trust	81
Expectations	83
Manifestation	85
Time	87
Change	89
Patience	91
Faith	93
Gratitude	95
Contentment	97
Happiness	99
Hope	101
Love	103
Forgiveness	105

Thoughts 107

Inspiration 109

Healing 111

Acceptance 113

Truth 115

Universal Love 117

Abundance 119

God's Love 121

8. Section 4 – Meditations 123

Open Your Heart 125

Remembering Home 127

Meet Your Guides 129

9. Section 5 – Reflections 133

Your Choice 135

Nature 137

Destination 139

A Peaceful Way 141

A Prayer for Oneself and Humanity 143

10. Conclusion 145

11. Acknowledgements 147

Introduction

Love Awakens You is an inspirational, self-help book. It gives you the tools to become a better you. It helps to unlock your true self and become a better version of yourself.

You begin to understand the difference between love and fear. This opens you up to new possibilities to unlock your true potential. Unlocking your true potential is a journey that not only helps you, but also helps others along the way. You become an inspiration for others by showing them a better way to be. As you learn to open yourself to your loving inspiration and guidance, you become your own inspiration. You begin to live a life of peace and happiness.

Your peace, happiness and self-confidence emanate from you and shows others the same is available to them. Your example of love shining from you, gives hope and courage to others that they too can be happy and peaceful.

Your journey as love awakens within you is one where you are helped along the way. This loving guidance always shows you the best way to be. It may seem strange at first to listen to advice from up above. As you become accustomed to hearing and following the advice, you realize life flows better and the ups and downs become less drastic.

Love Awakens You releases the chains that have kept you bound tightly within your limited prison. A prison where you are unable to spread your wings and soar. As you open to a new you, you begin to realize the unending support and love you have to help you. Helping you on a journey where you flower into a beautiful you. Free to be the person you so richly deserve.

Definitions

I use the term Holy Spirit to represent the source of my inspiration, guidance and intuition.

I use the term God to represent the source of all power.

I do not use these terms in a religious sense but only to represent a presence much greater than myself.

History

When I turned 16, that summer I was grounded (I got fired from a job for being sassy). I was only allowed to leave the house for a different small part-time job I got. Needless to say, I spent most of my 16th summer in my bedroom. In my bedroom I had a picture of Jesus. It was on an oval piece of wood and the edges still had the tree bark on it.

I spent a lot of time staring at the picture and drifting off into space. At the time, I did not realize that I was spending a whole lot of time with the angels and Jesus. I enjoyed my time with them, even if I did not understand that was what I was doing. I was only 16 after all!

As a teenager, there were two things I knew for sure about myself:

1. When I got older, I was going to a psychic.
2. I was going to move to the Southwest.

Both things came true.

Fast forward to my early 40's and I did go to see a psychic in Santa Fe. In her office, she had a large feather with a crystal underneath it. At the end of the session, I picked up the crystal (a beautiful citrine point) and the whole inside turned to liquid!

I immediately put it down and thought – I am not ready for this!

As I left her office and walking around afterwards, everything seemed so much clearer, brighter colors, and louder sounds. I saw things with more clarity. It was as if I was sleep walking before and now, I was awake. Granted the feeling only lasted a few days but it was amazing.

I called this psychic for a reading about six weeks later. At the end of the reading, she asked me if there was anything she could do for me. I said yes, and that she had this crystal which I had been thinking about. I described the crystal to her.

She said yes, that was the crystal. Then she told me this story. About a year earlier the crystal told her it no longer belonged to her and to bury it in the ground. She had just recently dug up the crystal just before my first session with her. She did not know who it was supposed to go to.

Since I had asked about the crystal, she said the crystal now belonged to me. She sent the crystal to me. This crystal opened the door to a whole new world. I mention this because from this first crystal – I found a person who taught a Spiritual Awareness class.

The Spiritual Awareness classes were to learn about chakras, crystals, how to read auras, how to do clairvoyant energy healings, and meet different beings. All these things seemed quite natural to me.

In my mid 40's I did move to the Southwest, which ended up being Arizona. Shortly after moving, I called my Spiritual Awareness instructor for a reading. She said that I was going to write inspirational sayings. She was very sure about this.

Even though she told me this, I was sure I was not going to write inspirational sayings. I did not like writing and I am not good with words. Besides, writing is hard work and takes a great deal of concentration. It was not going to happen!

I also took two crystal classes in Sedona. Well, that did it! I started buying crystals all the time. I was hooked. Crystals really did open me up to a most wonderous new world.

I also worked at a bookstore doing readings for people. While I was at the bookstore, Gary R. Renard's *The Disappearance of the Universe* book came out. The owner of the bookstore showed me the book but I was not interested in it.

As I was learning about spirituality, I would go to the larger bookstores to the New Age or Spiritual sections and look to see what popped out. I noticed *A Course in Miracles* book. I paused at it and then decided I did not need any miracles.

A couple of years later, a friend gave me *The Disappearance of the Universe* book. I started reading it and immediately knew I had to get *A Course in Miracles*.

So, I read *The Disappearance of the Universe*, *A Course in Miracles* and did the workbook in *A Course in Miracles* at the same time. I would not recommend this. It was tough. Let us just say my ego got really challenged!

At about the same time I was reading these two books, I found myself starting to write inspirational sayings and 4-line verses. An inspiration would come to me and I would write it down on whatever was available. Over the next couple of years, I had quite a collection of pieces of paper and various notebooks with lots of sayings and 4-line verses.

Sometimes I would wake up in the middle of the night with sayings coming to me. I would say to myself, I will remember it. Of course, I did not remember, so I started having a pen and paper nearby.

Things seemed to quiet down after a very busy couple of years. I went on with my life collecting crystals, doing crystal healings and writing a book titled *Cosmic Unity*.

So here I am in my mid 60's and, lo and behold, I am actually writing a book with inspirational sayings, 4-line verses, answers to questions you did not even know you had, meditations and reflections. Eighteen years ago, I would not have thought it possible that I would be writing a book for the upliftment of humanity.

Who knew?

Oh yeah – the Holy Spirit did!

How to use this Book

It is best to start reading Section 1, then Section 2, then Section 3. Reading the sections in the order presented helps to prepare you for the next section. Each section is opening you up to a new way of being.

Slowly is the key here. By going slowly, the effects of each section will have a long-lasting effect on you. Each section brings you deeper and deeper into an understanding of a new way to live.

Section 4 and Section 5 can be read at any time.

Section 1 is a compilation of inspirational sayings. The inspirational sayings are just that. Inspiration to help lift you up. To help you remember what it is like to be in a good mood all the time.

The sayings release the constant gnawing of the idea that you are not good enough. That no matter what you do, you will suffer in some way. The inspiration you get from the sayings will help to remind you that you are here to enjoy life.

Life in not meant to be hard. You are here to learn lessons but the learning does not have to be painful. You will always have lessons to learn, but you can learn them with ever expanding hope, ease and grace.

You can read the sayings in any order you like. It is preferable to read them in the order presented. The sayings are organized in a way to slowly open you up to a new way of being.

Read each saying slowly. It is best not to rush through them but to read 3 to 4 a day. You want to give yourself time to adjust to whatever happens in your journey to the light.

Section 2 is a collection of 4-line verses, which are more in-depth inspirational sayings. They are an interesting and different way of looking at life. The verses expand our awareness of what life is.

Our awareness becomes more grounded in knowing we are on the path of openness. The path to love's light is with open arms waiting to embrace us. To remind us we are innocent and all is forgiven.

Our storehouse of kindness is shown to us to encourage us along the way. To know we are following in the footsteps of those before us. The ones who now show us the way home.

Read each 4-line verse slowly. Enjoy the feeling you get from each one. You may want to only read two or three a day. This will allow you to reflect on the beauty of each verse.

Section 3 contains answers to questions you did not even know you had. It is best to read each answer in the order presented. Each of the answers intertwine with each other. They each present a piece of the puzzle.

As you read each answer, a piece of the puzzle is revealed and placed into a picture. A picture that shows the whole.

The answers from the beginning to end create a circle which brings you back to yourself. This circle of life is where you learn to remember who you really are.

The answers unlock your true potential. The potential of the choice you have in choosing love over fear. You have the power to become a shining beacon of light to inspire the lost souls to make the choice themselves. Your example gives hope to all.

It is best to read one answer a day and you may want take a few days rereading that answer. When ready, read the next answer. You may want to take one or more days rereading the next answer. Read the next one when you are ready and so forth. This gives you time to adjust to a new way of thinking. If you rush through the answers, you may feel overwhelmed. Going slowly gives you the time you need to become aware of a different way of living.

Section 4 contains meditations designed to help you relax and learn something about yourself. This learning will help guide you to the way of peace. The peace that all deserve to have.

Just before starting any of the meditations, ask to join with the Holy Spirit. By joining with the

Holy Spirit, the meditations will be more powerful. You will be shown and given exactly what you need.

If you forget to join with the Holy Spirit, the meditation will still be great. It just may not be as enlightening as it could have been.

There is no right or wrong in doing these meditations. It is what you choose to put into the meditation that determines what you get out of them.

Choose to do the meditations with an open heart and all will be revealed. As you are learning to open your heart, each time you do the meditations you flow with ease and grace. It becomes easier and more relaxing each time.

You begin to realize you have stayed hidden far too long. Go forth and share your joy at remembering who you really are. Help others to find their way back to a home never lost and never forgotten. Just misplaced, but soon to be rejoined with themselves.

Section 5 is a reflection of ideas for you to ponder. The reflections give you a choice of how you want to live your life. You can choose a life of love or a life of fear.

It is how we want to be remembered which gives us the impetus to learn to grow into a better person. Our growth does not come at a price. Our growth is only the beginning of a new way of living.

As we reflect upon how we want to be, let us remember we are here to help others and ourselves. To open to love's awareness that all are welcomed into love's embrace. We are the bringers of the dawn. The dawn of a new age.

Section 1 – Inspirational Sayings

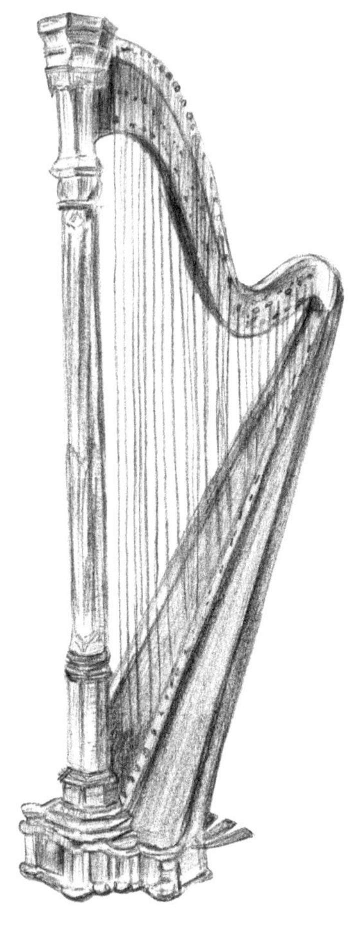

Love surrounds you

May you be blessed with love's light embrace

Join with love and become one with yourself

Live your light, and love will shine through

Come together and spread your wings

Come to yourself and love who you are

Disconnect from the world to truly know yourself

Allow your light within to shine through

If the truth be known, be one with yourself

Let the light of God be one with you

Choose the light way and all will fall into place

Trust the process and you will have what you need
when you need it

An open heart lets your light shine out

Time dissolves where love resides

Be heart centered to find your world of peace

Caress the waves of love to end the agony of emptiness

May your journey into the light find you at peace

Home is where the heart is, and the heart belongs to God

May your path be illuminated by light and love

May your light guide you on your journey into the depths of awareness

Happiness is the road to recovery

Surrender to the river of life

Rest gently in the wings that support you

If you never stop, how can you reflect upon yourself

For only that which is loved is free

Anything is possible, miracles do happen

Light extends beyond the realm of sight

Sing the song of love and sway in peace

Timelessness is beauty within

In the quiet of stillness, clarity comes

Release the chains that bind you

Hope is forever satisfied with God's love

Compassion is the way to oneness

Pearls of wisdom exist only when shared

Let the light of God remove all corners of darkness

The path of light is found by trusting your intuition

Gentle waves wash away the sorrow

In the emptiness, lies fullness

The beauty of a person's soul is seen through the heart not the eyes

Journey from the darkness into the light by opening to loves awareness

Heartfelt kindness heals all

The river of life ebbs and flows with the inspiration
of the great rays of love

A heart that is broken can be mended when you
share your love and light

Every moment is perfect with God

Be open to spirit and let the wings of change guide
you on your path

Beauty is the sight unseen

In death, life is renewed

God's love shines bright wherever you go

Time slows to a still moment when looked upon
with grace and compassion

The ocean of life grows deep within and blossoms
anew when nurtured with growing love

Where beauty resides, bounty replenishes

Inspiration is your soul guiding you to joy

Lessons are but learnt behavior

No one leaves you when they stay in your heart and mind

Shine bright upon all those whose love is growing

God is home and home is where you find yourself

Sometimes we choose the most difficult path but the most enlightening

Time moves on but love never changes

The quietest place on Earth is within

Let the shadows of life fall away

Life is not meant to be hard

The beauty within rumbles as it slowly awakens to love

Dance to the rhythm of your soul

Miracles are found within

Balance is found when duality is one

Rest in the wings that nurture you

The beauty of two souls remains intertwined throughout eternity

Open your heart and soul to the wonders of the world

In God's love, we find ourselves

Serenity is peacefulness found

Freedom comes from within yourself

To truly know oneself is to truly know God

The beauty within is the beauty without

Your star shines bright, and know that all who are touched by you are enlightened by you

May your journey into the depths of awareness be filled with light and laughter

Our power comes from the beauty we give

Timelessness is the goal

Our greatest growth comes from facing our greatest fear

Live life to the fullest by making God your most desire

Fear remains when you look outside yourself

Lessons are learned when you are no longer hiding

Judge not the world for you judge yourself

Dreams are desires manifest

Following the path of least resistance brings us closer to home

In the circle of life there is but a star for those who gave their lives

Duality is the curse of the despair

May the sparkle of the day come with dawn's new beginning

Only you can give yourself happiness

May the journey of your soul be blessed in love
and light

There is nothing but love upon which all things
rest

We do not know what we are doing except for the
love of God

May you always be blessed with the truth of love

Connectedness joins us all as one

25

The seed of darkness will dissolve when you open
your heart

The light of the world is your beauty within

It is never boring to be with yourself

May your heart sing with joy at all the love that
surrounds you

Awaken dear ones, to the dawn of a new way

The gift of immortality - God's love

Forgiveness is the way

Section 2 – 4-Line Verses

Cindi Buckley

May the light touch your soul
May laughter touch your heart
May joy touch your life
May love touch us all

See with your heart
Hear with your heart
Feel with your heart
To know love

Open to a new way of being
Open to a most wonderous world
Open to a bubble of beauty
Open to a new way of sharing

But for the peace of God, I rise above to the heavens
To be found among the strangers of love
To be anointed to the ways of light
Bringer of truth to the souls of lost

The stars up above shine bright
The sun shines down upon all
The glimmer of hope peeks through
The brightness of love encompasses all

Together we are on this journey
May the joy of life bless us all
When we meet again in the light of love
Where all our sins are dissolved

The river flows unending
The seas gentle waves caress
The ocean gives life abundance
The rain renews all

Heavy hearts close the dark
Light hearts open the dark
Darkness blinds the heart
Lightness binds the love

Life is love
Love is laughter
Laughter is joy
Joy is home

No one can do anything alone
Everyone can do everything
Anyone can do all
We all are one

Tear down the broken wall
Let it crumble to the ground
Pile high the broken debris
Blow away the broken crumbled debris

Float high above the skies
Soar around in spiral circles
Dive down the wind tunnel
Into the breeze of life

May the Lord show you the way home
To the abundance that awaits you
To the light and love of God's promised way
To be one with all

Release the past
Love yourself
Look forward to the future
Future is now

In the darkness you see the light
In the silence you hear the angels sing
In the light you see your beauty's reflection
In the song you hear the one true voice reminding
you of who you are

May the stars light your way
May your dreams come true
May your imagination be filled with wonder and awe
May you always be surrounded by love and light

Let there be light where darkness resides
Let there be love where stillness resides
Let there be peace where calmness exists
Let there be openness where truth is

Shed this old and weathered shell
Expand the light beyond the boundaries
you have made
Grow into the shining beacon of light you are
Be the sparkling star in your Father's eye

Cindi Buckley

The storm clouds hide
The wind breezes away
The rain cleans
The sun shines bright

Bodies join into one
Hearts meld as one
Minds become one
Love becomes all

Time moves forward
Time moves backward
Time stands still
Time no longer is

Tell me where to go
Tell me when to go
Tell me how to go
Tell me why to go

Lost souls wander
Lost spirit found
Lost hearts broken
Lost love abounds

The stars sparkle bright
The moon glow grows
The sun shines forth
The light grows great

Cindi Buckley

Where shadows reside, darkness hides
Where light abides, love resides
Where joy shines, laughter abides
Where kindness lives, beauty is

The beauty within glows bright
Its warmth showers you with love
Peace and joy surround you
The elixir of life is yours to behold

Embers burn
Flames flare
Water gushes
Love flowers

Past never was
Tomorrow is never sure
Today is now
Now is all there is

Darkness embraces the soul
Shadow encompasses the spirit
Light embraces the mind
Love encompasses all

Time is still
Ripples in water
Dew drops hang
Life is forever

Cindi Buckley

Joined hearts are never apart
Love blossoms where flowers grow
Time passes into infinity
We shall meet again where space and time are one

Rocks are hard
Water is fluid
Flow over the bumps
Rise above the ebb of your life

Stand tall
Stand firm
Stand rooted
Stand in love

Two souls as one
Birds intertwine
Trees circle
Two souls merge

Ancient wisdom abounds in the land
Knowledge exists in the space in between
Truth resides within yourself
Love binds all together

Let the wind carry your worries away
Let the sun warm your soul
Let the water wash you clean
Let the earth energize you

May you be blessed with serenity
May you be blessed with peacefulness
May you be blessed with timelessness
May you be blessed with hearts joined

The angels are singing your praise
The angels are gently swaying in the breeze
The angels are heralding you home
The angels are lighting the way to yourself

Awake my child from your slumbering sleep
Awake to the dawn of a new day
Awake to the remembrance of yourself
Awake to knowing you are loved

Section 3 – Answers

Home

Home has never been lost, yet it needs to be remembered. You have forgotten where you truly belong. You have separated from your family.

You have chosen to walk your path alone. You believe you are able to do anything and everything by yourself. You believe you can do no wrong.

Home is where your brothers and sisters are. Where your family of support is. It is where there is a free-flowing exchange of ideas. Where you help each other in all ways.

Home is the sharing of love to help uplift each other. Where you encourage each other to be better versions of yourselves. Home is the entourage of souls intertwined in love's embrace.

It is where you remember what you have lost. You remember the camaraderie, the laughter and the smiles. You remember what it is like to have support. Support for who you truly are. Support for your generous ways, and support for your gracious ideas.

Home reminds you; you are not alone. Home is the rejoining of yourself to a place you never left. To a way of life, you have forgotten. It reminds you; you are an integral part of family.

Your family is lost without you. Your rebellion has taught you; you cannot do anything alone. You need to be home where your love and support are.

Once you choose to return home, all imagined bad things that happened fade away into a distant memory. The memory never to return.

Home is where you are your true self. A loving, kind, compassionate person. A person who now has the support to go forth and teach love. To teach others home is where they belong.

Independence

There is no independence. No one can do anything alone. No one is ever alone. Now, you may think you are alone but there are legions of souls waiting to help you. You also have many guides who help you along the way.

All these souls and guides are seen and unseen. You may dismiss this idea because you believe that you are independent of anyone and anything. You believe by doing whatever, by yourself, gives you strength to carry on.

Actually, by believing you are independent, you drain yourself of the energy to sustain yourself. You lose the ability to see clearly and to hear the loving guidance you so richly deserve. You become clouded with a false sense of self-righteousness.

Independence is the crying child left alone in a world full of busyness. The child who has to learn to fend for itself. The child is lost, alone and has no one to help it.

The aloneness is a desperate feeling of abandonment. Where the child feels no one cares or loves it. So, it picks itself up by its boot straps and carries on. Knowing that relying on anyone will only lead to disappointment.

The child believes independence is the only way to ensure it will never be disappointed, hurt or truly alone. Independence teaches survival of the fetus is the only way to be safe. It teaches that you are the only one to count on.

You cannot count on anyone else to help you. You determine the best way to proceed is to remain aloof. Acting like you do not care about anyone or anything. Your independence has protected you from ever being hurt.

Yet inside you, you are crying for attention and affection. Deep down you feel alone and wonder - has independence lead you on the wrong path? Does independence really have your best interests at heart?

Maybe, you begin to realize independence is not a healthy way to live. Maybe, maybe there is someone out there who cares for me and wants to help me. Let me take a tentative step towards trusting that help is around the corner.

Let me begin to realize I am not alone and I do not have to do everything and anything on my own. I do not have to rely on the strength of myself which drains me of my vital source of refreshment. There are legions of souls who are there to help me.

Let me learn to ask for help and know that I am always surrounded by love.

Individuality

Individuality is the belief you are separate from everyone and everything. Your individuality is of the upmost importance to you. You believe being an individual gives you the power to be special. There is no one else like you.

Your thoughts, words and actions only belong to you. No one else has ever thought or done the things you have done. You are the only one who has any particular idea. No one else could possibly think the same as you.

Your individuality limits you. It limits you because you are not open to a new or different way of thinking. You restrict yourself by binding yourself to smallness.

Individuality is the death of oneness. It reminds us we are not open to love. You are not open to becoming a better you.

Individuality reinforces separateness. It reinforces we do not need another's help. It reinforces being alone is the only way to be sure, we never need be disappointed by another.

Individuality is the curse of the damned. It is the way down the dark tunnel never to see the light of day. It is the ropes tightening around you causing burns and scrapes. It is the wrecking of who you really are.

Individuality need not be the death of you. It only needs to be recognized that you are not an individual but part of the whole. You believe giving up your individuality will be the death of what makes you unique.

You are loved by God, as is everyone else loved by God. You all are joined in love. As you learn you are not an individual, you begin to see and feel the well-wishes of all.

You begin to become a part of the whole. You learn everyone is a part of the whole. You learn everyone is trying to do their best.

You cannot do your best as long as you believe you are an individual. You only do your best when you are willing to acknowledge a presence greater than yourself. You learn to trust the Holy Spirit for guidance.

This remembrance brings home the idea you are never alone. Once you remember this, you feel encouraged to continue on this path. You are sure you are on the way home.

Comparison

When you compare yourself to another you are belittling yourself into nothingness. You feel as though you are unimportant because you have not accomplished as much as another. You feel useless because you are not out in the world getting other people's admiration. You feel poor because you do not have as much as another.

You compare yourself to another by lording over them that you have more than them. You are doing more than them by doing more in the world; therefore, you are better than they are. The comparisons go on endlessly.

You can even compare yourself to yourself. You compare yourself to yourself by saying last time you did this, so this time you will do that. You constantly want better things. You constantly want to prove yourself to yourself and to others.

The 'Ring Around the Rosie' of comparisons makes you die a slow death. You are swallowed up in the fury of frantic comparisons. You must strive for more and more.

Comparison of any kind is not healthy. It is not healthy to be always putting yourself down. This reinforces feeling bad about yourself. It reminds you; you are unworthy.

Comparisons create a seesaw effect of up and down feelings. This is no way to live. You are better than this. You are an integral part of the whole. Without you, all is lost.

Every person here is just as important as every other person. It does not matter what you do for a living. It does not matter how much you own. What does matter is you are kind and compassionate to all who cross your path.

Comparisons become less often when you accept you are important to the whole. Without you the whole is broken into pieces like a jigsaw puzzle. Slowly the pieces come back together.

Comparison to yourself and to others drifts away. You begin to see you are all the same. You are all looking to find love. Love is found when you join with the Holy Spirit.

The need to belittle yourself into nothingness has disappeared. You rise to shine high above the clouds. Your radiant self has arrived to spread the word. There is no longer any need to compare yourself to yourself or to others.

Competition

Are you in competition with yourself or with other people? Competition of either kind is destructive to you. It makes you feel inferior.

It makes you feel as if you are never going to be good enough for anything. You strive for an outcome which will make you feel good about yourself. The only outcome you can be sure of is that what happens has already been decided.

Decided not by you or other people but decided by the invisible hand that directs your every step. Which invisible hand do you listen to? Do you follow the invisible hand that says, 'Pummel them into submission' or do you listen to the invisible hand that says 'We are here to enjoy ourselves, let's have fun!'?

Yes, you can have fun while pretending to be in competition with others. Pretend to be in competition with others but be sure to remember no one wins and no one loses.

The only loss there is, is when you flaunt your win over another. You also lose when you get angry you did not come out on top. Either way you feel bad about yourself.

You can have competition with yourself. You decide you are going to strive to improve yourself to the point of competing. You go so far one time and then you push yourself to go further. You push yourself to the breaking point.

The breaking point is where you start to crumble into a heap of 'I cannot do this!'. This type of competition is internal and unseen by prying eyes. You feel better knowing you are not competing with others.

The internal or external competition is just as destructive. Both remind you to strive for more and more. The more you gain, the more you have.

What is it you are really gaining? Do you gain peace? Do you gain contentment? Does competition help you to be sure of yourself? Does competition harbor a growing love for yourself and others?

Competition drags you down into the dregs of darkness. To be whiplashed into believing it has the power to show you the way. It keeps you on high alert to always find a way to reinforce your superiority over others.

Competition is not the way. No one is better than another. We are all here to help each other. We cannot do that as long as we harbor feelings of superiority or inferiority.

Help is on the way. Help to realize we are all one. We are all striving to remember who we really are. All we need to do is ask for help from the loving hand that guides us.

Conflict

Conflict makes you feel alive. It gives you a jolt of energy to continue to push forward. It makes you strong.

Strength in conflict comes from ourselves. We are the ones pushing out the battle between two wills. We want to fight with another to feel alive.

The feeling conflict gives is that of the hero to the rescue. You will show them how it is done. How to win, even if someone else becomes hurt.

Is this any way to live? To hurt another so you feel better about yourself. To reinforce the battle between person or persons known or unknown.

Or, does conflict make you run and hide? Afraid to stand up for yourself. Afraid you will get hurt physically, emotionally or mentally.

By hiding, conflict cannot find you. You stay hidden all the while the festering anger is growing inside you. Until one day you become the aggressor and lash out.

You lash out and realize there was nothing to fear about conflict. It makes you feel strong and in control. You are now the reigning supremacy.

The cycle of conflict is never ending. Only you can break it by realizing there is a better way. A way to not hurt others or yourself.

What is there to fight about anyway? The trinkets this world has to offer. The lack of supplies or lack of sharing resources. You can choose to help resolve these issues by giving up conflict.

When you give up conflict, you help to find a peaceful solution that benefits all. Be sure to address your resistance to the idea that everyone deserves all. We are all in the same boat.

We are all afraid to share what is best for all. We think by doing this we are giving up something that belongs only to us. We are not the only ones to hold onto an unhealthy way of thinking.

Giving up conflict means you are willing to become a beacon of light. To show others you honor their journey and are willing to help others to find their way from conflict. You realize conflict damages you by reinforcing the struggle for power.

A power that does not belong to you. It is a power that drives you into despair. It is a false power.

True power comes from within. It is the strength of love in knowing you are here to share the message of love. Love heals all and conflict fades into wisps of ribbons floating away never to return.

Judgement

When you judge others, you are judging yourself. Anything you think about others is what you think of yourself. Judgement is a rigid pole not to be veered from. Once made, never to be reversed.

The reflection of yourself in others is how you learn. You either learn fear or you learn love. It is so easy to judge others thinking they are the problem, not you.

Judgement of any kind hurts you in ways unbeknownst to you. It keeps you rooted to power you think you have over others. Judgement makes you feel big and strong and in control.

Be not deceived into thinking your judgment justifies your way of thinking. Thinking you are superior over others, and that you know how to fix what is wrong with everyone else.

This judgement drives us into the ground. It tightens around us and keeps us buried in the depths of denial. The denial that we have chained ourselves to misery.

We want people to join us in our misery. It justifies our feelings and keeps us feeling brave. Brave to continue judging others and to get others to follow our path of destruction.

This judgment shows us we were right all along. Judgement of this kind is not inspiration, it is destructive. It reinforces your belittlement and shows how small you really are. That you need to create a following of depressed and lost souls.

Jump out of this type of judgement and skip into the open doorway of your soul. Judgement of any kind reduces you to nothingness. You are not nothingness; you are love's way to the shining beacon of peace.

Release judgement and know that peace awaits you. The peace you find gives you the strength to continue in a more loving, kind way.

Denial

Denial is an overwhelming tour de force. It is strong and holds its grip on you. It acts like death if you were to ever acknowledge it.

Denial reinforces the philosophy "you were wrong and I was right". It teaches us how to lie and come out as a savior. The reigning royalty has arrived to save the day.

When you are in denial, you are hiding from yourself. You are running away like a scared little child. Hiding under the bed afraid the monsters are going to catch you.

Yet, the monster is denial. It has already caught you and weaved its web of deceit into your every fiber of being. It gives you the feeling of being in control.

In control of what? What is it you need control over? The lack of acknowledgement of denial is denial itself.

Denial rains false bravado, which give you the reinforcement you are doing right. It reminds you that you are feeling good, but this is temporary and, is due to your refusal to know you are responsible for yourself.

No one else is responsible for your thoughts, words and actions. Only you are. Denial keeps hidden who you really are.

You reinforce your temporary, fleeting feeling of supremeness by denying you are worthy of love. Your worthiness comes from who you really are. You are the embodiment of light. Light which is meant to be shared.

Let denial in and you have lost to the ugly world of fear. Fear that you may be seen for who you really are. Afraid that you will be ridiculed and teased for being open with your light.

Nothing is further from the truth. The truth is you are a leader in the war against fear. You are to shine your light for those lost in denial. You are to help them find their way out of the depths of denial.

Denial is strong and its vise-like grip reminds us we are weak and cannot survive without hiding. Hiding from being our true selves is lacking in imagination. Imagination that we are the embodiment of truth itself.

Anger

You are never angry at another person; you are only angry at yourself. Each person you meet is a reflection of yourself. While they may seem different in so many ways, they are not different from your soul self.

You use other people to displace your anger, so you do not have to take responsibility for yourself. It was their fault and they are to blame for your problem. A problem that they caused because they did not listen to you.

Now you are justified in being angry with them. This relieves you from having to be kind to them. You no longer need to be civil to them. You only have to tolerate their presence. You tolerate their presence with a snubbed shoulder and barely a kind word.

All this anger you have for another is the anger you have for yourself. You are afraid to deal with the issue that caused you to be angry. You do not want to look at that part of yourself.

You might see something ugly and horrendous. You cannot deal with the fact you have been the one to cause the anger. It is easier to blame another for your troubles.

All the anger is clouding your judgement. You cannot see clearly with a heart full of anger. All you see is the red streaks bleeding down into a world buried in pain and suffering.

You caused this. You made this world you now live in. You are proud of yourself for what you have created. You created this all by yourself. Didn't you do good!

Anger never resolves anything. It only reinforces bad behavior. It does not help others or yourself. It only drags you down below the waterline where you drown in your sorrows.

Replace anger with forgiveness. The type of forgiveness where you understand no one has done anything wrong. All are innocent.

Forgiveness opens the door to love. Love awakens when you decide there is a better way to live. Let love guide you on your way to peace. Peace for all is everyone's right.

Pain

Pain is present when guilt is around. Guilt is a secret buried deep in the past of a time long forgotten. The echoes of pain remain.

You suffer physically with the constant punishment of the body. The body will age but you can age gracefully. Proper nourishment is essential to release pain.

Nourishment of the mind by love's guiding hand teaches us to honor our heavenly way. We let pain seep in the crevices and cracks of our crumbling wall. The wall we built to keep pain out.

Yet pain continues to flourish in the recesses of our mind. We remember the hurts others have caused and blame them for our pain. We suffer a fool's journey by believing we can control the pain we feel.

There is no control of pain, only release of guilt. The punishment we give ourselves becomes comfortable. It becomes normal and we believe that this is the only way to live.

It is not! Love's enduring and steady guidance reminds us that pain is something we do to ourselves. Any source of discomfort is pain. We can release ourselves from pain by opening our hearts to love's abiding joy.

Do you believe you are worthy of love? Do you believe you are here to suffer? Do you believe you deserve better?

Of course, you are worthy of love. Of course, you are not here to suffer. Of course, you deserve better.

You but have to choose to step into love's light. By choosing to step into love's light you are honoring your true self. The part of you where you remember to be kind and compassionate to yourself. Where you learn to share your kindness and compassion, which will diminish the pain and discomfort you feel.

Pain becomes a distant memory to be forgotten when we ensure we embrace the flowering glimmer of love. Love guides us on a journey where the ebb and flow of pain become smooth and steady. The steadiness of love endures and releases pain to where it belongs.

Pain belongs not to us but to a distant memory best forgotten. Let the memory fade and be replaced with peace and serenity of love. Let the light of love show you the way to a peaceful existence.

Doubt

Do you doubt yourself? Absolutely! You doubt yourself of every minute of every day. You doubt you will be able to function within the given guidelines of society's rules and regulations.

Rules and regulations that were put in place to keep you safe. Safe from yourself and others. Yet, you know somewhere, somehow, there is a better way. Deep down inside you there is a rumble of discontentment.

The rumble is growing but you do not know what it is. The rumble gives you doubt, doubt that there is a better way. Yet, you decide to pursue what the rumble is. You want to let the discontentment transform into something better.

You take a small step towards the rumble and you find you did not run away in fear. This is the first step to walking your way out of the straight and narrow path of confinement. Your doubt begins to collapse in on itself. The black hole of discontentment is shrinking.

You begin to have more confidence in yourself. Your doubt begins to lessen. Your tentative step towards the rumble now becomes a firm step. Slowly you are gaining the ability to be sure of yourself.

How did you do this? You decided doubt was destroying your life. You were always in fear of something or someone. That fear was crippling you to the point where you were hunched over and bent into a crumpled heap of yourself.

Stand straight and take the step forward. Remember who you are. You are the light of the world. The one who is to show others they can dig their way out of the hole they dug for themselves.

Doubt is the destroyer of faith. Faith that you are the most important helper in this world. While you still have to follow all the rules and regulations of the world, you can still light the way for others.

Discontentment will be replaced with contentment. Doubt will diminish when you learn there is nothing to fear. Walk the path of light and all will be revealed.

Fear

Fear is hidden in the recesses and folds of time long gone. It is a remembrance of what once was. It is where we bring back the memories of a scared little one.

You believe yourself to be small and insignificant. Scared to be seen and heard. Afraid to be noticed in a world gone mad. Yet all the while wanting some form of recognition that you are here.

You want to belong to a world where fear rules the day. Where fear dictates you must hide and run yet somehow you need to be noticed. You want to be bigger than life. You want to show the world you exist and what you say and do is right and justified.

You let fear in to give you the courage to stand up for yourself. You feel the power and it makes you strong. Stronger than you ever thought you could be.

Then you are slapped down by someone who is bigger and better than you. You run and hide to lick your wounds. Vengeance is yours and fear gives that to you.

Fear tells you to go and get your revenge. You deserve it because you have been wronged. You need to prove to yourself that you cannot be bested by anyone.

Yet this cycle of fear is never ending unless you choose to realize you can break it. Break the whirlwind cycle of vengeance by realizing you are not alone. Help is but a thought away.

Ask for help to step away from fear and help will be given. Help is always but a request away. You only need to ask. Remembering to ask is the challenge.

When you are uncomfortable in any way, ask to remember love. The see-saw, up and down, back and forth, fear to love, effect may be a bit uncomfortable at first.

Persevere and love will melt away fear's hold on you. You will remember the good times and peace will return. Peace to realize you are not little and insignificant but an integral part of love's abiding way.

Ego

Ego is the embodiment of fear and fear has many names. It is hidden in the reaches of our mind far beyond the grasp of sanity. Ego is where we lose to fear.

Fear presents itself in ways not known. Hidden in the recesses of a cloaked world. The world we believe will bring our salvation.

Salvation cannot be found where darkness reigns. It rains broken teardrops weeping with blood for all to see. Darkness takes hold and teaches us to defend ourselves with vicious intent.

This is not the way. Ego tells us we need to be superior to others, control others and make others do our bidding. By this, we prove to ourselves we are on the right path.

We tell ourselves we are on the path of righteousness by proving to ourselves we deserve to be in control. We know what is best for everyone. Ego has given us the power to do this.

But what ego does not tell you is that by giving your power to it – you lose yourself. You lose yourself to agony and despair. Nothing is ever good enough.

You simply need more and more to satisfy your insatiable need to be right. By being right, you justify your means to an end. You have delivered the Holy Grail of immortality to yourself.

Is this the price you want to pay? Do you want to sacrifice your peace for small trinkets of nothingness? By releasing the ego to the Holy Spirit, you regain peace and serenity.

Ego is devious and will try to regain its control over you. It has subtle ways to show you it is the only path to follow. Be vigilant, my dear ones, for your path to sanity is only found through love.

Sanity is returned when you bid farewell to jealously, anger, annoyance, uncomfortableness, gossip, guilt and the many ways ego entices you to return to its fold. Once sanity has returned, peace, love and happiness are yours to behold.

Wounds are healed and the open sores of hurt are closed. Your collection of eons of memories of betrayals are but wisps of thoughts once healed. No longer to be focused on or remembered.

Ego has faded into the winds to be replaced by love's embrace. Where the wings of love surround you with safety in knowing all is well.

Control

You have no control. Lest you think you have control over yourself or others, you do not. You are either being ruled by the ego or guided by the Holy Spirit.

You only have two choices. You can choose love or you can choose fear. Depending on your choice, depends on how much control there is over your thoughts, emotions and actions.

If you are being ruled by the ego, then you are living in fear. You believe you can control any outcome. The ego lives for throwing curve balls at you. It wants to constantly shake things up, so you are never sure of what can happen.

The ego lives off pain and misery. Reminding you – you are in control of what happens. How can that be? Given the ego is your master. Master of fear and you run to ego for safety from the uncertain.

The ego now has full control over you. Since you ran to it, it tells you, it is the only thing to believe in. You are not in control, ego is.

You can choose a different path. The path to being guided by the Holy Spirit. The Holy Spirit will never try to control you. However, you must always ask for assistance in any endeavor you undertake. Without asking, the Holy Spirit cannot help.

There is no control here, only guidance. You can try to do whatever on your own, struggling and straining to solve the problem. Learning to ask for help is the first step to giving up false control. When giving up false control, you gain confidence, peace and surety.

You become more accepting of different ways of doing things. You are asking for help in all the right ways. By asking for the loving hand to guide you, you are giving up fear.

Giving up fear is hard at first. You have become comfortable living in a certain way. But fear only keeps you from your true radiant self.

There may be times when you question the validity of your choice to choose love. Know this; love will always guide you, never control you. You are here to remember your one true home.

As long as you think you have control, life will be hard. The only control you have is to choose love or choose fear. The choice you make determines which path you walk.

Which path do you want to walk? The one that leads to pain and suffering or the one that leads to serenity, peace and calmness.

Duality

Duality has many names. Night-day, hot-cold, high-low, right-left, light-dark, up-down, yin-yang, back-forth, right-wrong, love-fear, etc. Anything that has an opposite is duality. Everything here in this world has an opposite.

Duality is where you learn about yourself. You learn either fear or love. You learn to follow the path which guides you to the most loving outcome. The most loving outcome is the one which is best for all.

Duality keeps you divided from others and yourself. You find that there is never a good solution to whatever problem you have. The back and forth of what should be done is never satisfied.

You find yourself on a roller-coaster ride of emotions. The highs and lows of your life become normal. The strain of never knowing what outcome will happen.

Duality keeps you rooted in the benign, the bland and narrow way of being. It may seem exciting to you to have the ups and downs giving you a jolt of excitement. This is a false sense of excitement. It does not last and needs constant renewing.

The constant renewing and reminders of duality keep you tied to fear. You need to be reminded you are not fear, but love. The only way out of duality is by loving yourself and all others.

Duality ends when you give up the need to feel charged up when there is a disagreement. Duality ends when you stop using another to make yourself feel better. Duality ends when you are ready to accept your part in helping all to awaken to a new day.

A new day that brings joy and peace and calmness to you. A day turns into a week which turns into a month. The bumps along the way become smaller and smaller. You are able to handle the bumps with ease, realizing you have a constant companion with you.

You are never alone and your constant companion will always guide you to the most loving, kind solution. Duality fades away to be replaced with love. Love has never left you. Duality only temporarily masked the light within you.

Death

Death is the desperate act of trying to save oneself. No one needs saving, as we are already saved. We do however need to understand that while we are already saved, we still need to work at breaking the cycle of birth and death.

Time churns the rotating cycle of life. It revolves around the never-ending cycle of death. As we return over and over, we begin to see how false life here is.

Death is a means to an end where we believe we have separated from our one true home. We have not! Our hearts desire is to be free. Free from the tyranny of the belief that our only goal here is to do whatever we must to not die. Yet death comes in many forms.

Physical death, emotional death, mental death and spiritual death. We die each time we betray ourselves by fighting to save what little we think we own. Fear of losing something, fear of losing anything, fear of losing our masks.

We believe that if we were seen as we really are, someone or something will kill us. Killing the embers of the growing flame of remembrance. Death comes swiftly to us as we let our guard down and let death take hold.

We hold onto the fear using it as a springboard to defend ourselves. We need to be the aggressor to show we are in control. We have the bravado to stand above all.

As we stand tall, death takes hold. Reminding us that we are but a small, insignificant speck of dust. Yet death shows us that there is a way out. It says follow me and you will be rewarded with riches you never dreamed of.

Do not follow! Death is a deceiver. It promises riches which it cannot deliver. This is only to entice you to follow a path far beyond where you belong. You belong where life is teeming with unbroken promises.

Life renewed releases death to where it belongs, buried beyond the reaches of time. Where time and space meet, there is life.

Death belongs to no one. It's never ending, unfolding cycle can be broken when you become the light and love of God.

Enemies

Do you have enemies? The answer is yes. Anyone who does not agree with you or your way of doing things, is your enemy.

You decided long ago if you were not the shining star in people's eyes, then they were not worthy of your time or effort. You made an enemy of them. You only want to be the leader who directs the puppets in the play.

Your enemy is the one who shows you how mean you are. They show you the angry eyes of betrayal. You are justified in having enemies because they caused you harm in some way.

You reinforce this behavior by dismissing them as you would swat a fly. They are menial and not worthy of you. Everyone is worthy of everyone. This is how you learn to turn your enemy into a friend.

Every person shows you where you are in the belief of enemies. Not everyone is going to be a fan of yours. Just because someone is not a fan of yours, does not mean you have to make an enemy of them.

What it does mean is you start to learn to accept that whoever you believed is an enemy is really someone showing you the way home. This person/

enemy is giving you the opportunity to show you a different way of thinking. To begin to take a step away from the belief that you have enemies.

Be sure to recognize when you are making someone an enemy by how you think of them. Are your thoughts about them loving? Are you accepting they have their own journey? Are you willing to forgive yourself and them, when you argue or show them hatred?

The angels sing, heralding you both home, when you decide they are no longer your enemy. Your enemy is now your friend. Long remembered stains of blood are now transformed into the light. Your enemy is no more and you are on your way home.

Specialness

Specialness is the sin of the deprived. It says you are the only one who has this or that. You are the only one to say or do something original. Something that no one else has done.

Specialness lets you walk around feeling untouchable. You are the chosen one. The one to teach others how to be.

You have been given special powers which only you have. You lord it over everyone because you are the supreme being. Specialness lets you know you stand high above everyone else.

Isn't it lonely up there? All by yourself, showing off. Making others jealous and wishing they were you. This specialness deprives you of peace. It creates contempt and listlessness.

As you wander the earth, showing off your specialness, you are losing your ability to remember you are not alone. Surprisingly, you find that there is someone else who parallels you and your powers.

What now? You are no longer special and you have lost your strength to continue. Specialness deprives you of the need to learn humility.

Humility is the way of the peaceful ones. It says everyone is special and everyone has a purpose here. Not to be special but to share our knowledge and encourage those who need encouragement.

We encourage others to be better than they are now. To embrace the loving way. To be shown that in the perceived loss of specialness, they actually gain the ability to become one with others.

Once you become one with others, you become more than the whole. You are the whole. Your awareness expands into the all-knowing. You realize specialness was binding you to the little and insignificant.

You no longer are little and significant. You are big and full and complete. The specialness you have held tight onto is now released into the wings of a butterfly. As you transform yourself from the cocoon into the butterfly, you become real.

You know in your heart that everyone is special. Everyone has a part to play in this never-ending cycle of crisscrossing roads. Your part is to show the way to ending the belief that only one person is special.

All are special and all are gifts to each other. We help each other. That is what we do.

Responsibility

You are responsible for yourself. You are responsible for the way you think, the words you say and the actions you do. No one else is responsible for anything you think, say or do.

This is hard to accept. It is much easier to blame another for all your troubles. It is easier to remove yourself from any responsibility for what happens to you. You believe you are never responsible for what happens.

Nothing could be further from the truth. As you blame others, you condemn them to be your slave. You are showing others how to behave badly. You are putting your guilt onto others.

You have decided being right is much more important than being happy. While you think you know what it takes to be happy – you do not! You think being right makes you happy.

Being right does not make you happy. It only gives you a false supremeness. A supremeness which makes you feel big.

This bigness is actually smallness. You have chosen to side with ego. You have chosen to make another person feel bad about themselves. You have chosen to treat others as disposable tools for you to manipulate.

Is this taking responsibility for yourself? Are you teaching others how to be responsible for themselves? Are you showing others how to treat others?

As long as you do not take responsibility for yourself. You are heading in the wrong direction. You are driving away from happiness. You are running away from yourself.

To be responsible means you are ready to accept yourself. You are ready to grow and learn what it means to be happy. You are ready to realize you are here to help others. You bloom into the beautiful person you really are.

Trust

Who do you trust? Do you trust yourself, someone else, the ego, or the Holy Spirit?

The typical thought about trust is that trust is earned. By earning trust, you have shown yourself to be an upstanding person. A person who earns trust by showering others with words they want to hear.

You have learned to placate a person's needs by giving flowery praises in order to get the attention you crave. You think by giving a person what they think they need, earns you, their trust. Once you have their trust, you believe you can do whatever you want and they will still trust you.

This is not trust. It is manipulation. You have manipulated another for your own selfish needs. The need to be the hero. To gain notoriety and be remembered for the person who satisfied another's emotional sadness.

You do not know what trust is. Trust is given, not earned. Only when you give trust and expect absolutely nothing in return, do you begin to understand what trust is.

When you give trust, you are telling the other person you believe in them. You are giving them the opportunity to believe in themselves. You are helping them to realize there is a better way than manipulating others.

There may be others you come across that constantly want to manipulate you, regardless of how much trust you give. The best you can do is wish them well and for as long as you are in contact with them, you still give trust. You want to help them be a better version of themselves.

The process of giving trust is hard. Trusting yourself, someone else or the ego leads you down the path of waywardness. You listlessly sway in a never-ending circle of false heroism.

You want to be the hero. Be the hero by trusting that the Holy Spirit guides you to the most suitable outcome for all. As you are guided to the most loving outcome, trust you are helping others in ways you do not know.

It is not up to you to know how giving trust will affect another. Only that it will. Maybe not this lifetime, maybe not the next, but it will help. While you are learning to trust, kindness begins to shine through.

Kindness and compassion are results of trust. When you say kind words to another, it is the kindness they remember, not the empty words to illicit feelings of idolism. As long as you trust with no expectations, then manipulation fades away.

Trust the Holy Spirit to always guide you on the path of love and light.

Expectations

Expectations kill inspiration. It does not allow for the free-flowing exchange of information. You expect something and get disappointed when you do not get it.

You have determined what it is you want. Therefore, you expect to get it. You cannot expect to get what you want and then be rewarded with pearls of wisdom.

Expectations set the stage for failure. Your determination to get what you want binds you to chains of hunger. Hunger is the desire to satisfy your want for whatever you expect.

You expect other persons to behave in a certain manner. When they do not, you lash out at them. Your expectation has not been met and it is their fault.

You have a set of expectations for everything. You have already determined what is supposed to happen. If it does not happen as you planned, you get frustrated. Your anger starts to boil over and you shut down the channels of awareness.

Expectations are a long-held belief that you deserve whatever it is you want. The belief that you know what is best for yourself. The belief that you can control all situations.

What is there to control? You have learned you cannot control others. You can only control your reaction to others.

By letting the Holy Spirit guide your reactions in uncomfortable situations, you are reopening the channels to awareness. You find your expectations are no longer. You begin to enjoy life more by realizing expectations have bound you to the chains of unhappiness.

Releasing expectations, in turn, gives you the freedom to feel open and clear. It allows you to be open to new possibilities. Possibilities you would never have accepted.

You now are free to explore a new way of thinking. A new way of approaching an idea. A new way of being.

Manifestation

Manifestation is not about getting things, obtaining more currency, or having more than another. It is about being one with the Holy Spirit. If you are one with the Holy Spirit, then what is best for yourself, will be best for all.

This is different way of thinking than how most people think. Our society is based on competition and conflict. About having more than another person. This is the philosophy of win-lose instead of win-win.

With the win-lose thought pattern, there will be someone who has a sense of lack. That lack makes a person feel inadequate, incomplete and insufficient. These feelings will manifest into a non-loving behavior. That person will lash out and sabotage themselves and others. They will not feel like they deserve feeling well, happy or being loved.

This is a never-ending cycle of fear. The fear becomes all encompassing, whereby driving your emotions into the depths of darkness. The darkness is deep-seated. It pushes you into despair and agony. The feeling of hopelessness sinks you further into fear.

How do you get out of this deep-seated fear? You join with the Holy Spirit to manifest what is best for yourself. Only when you join with the Holy Spirit does your fear diminish. It is important here to remember that what is best for yourself will always be what is best for all – when you join with the Holy Spirit.

Sometimes you will be given something in the physical and sometimes you will not. Remember that it is the Holy Spirit that knows what is best for you. Since when do we really know what it is we want? You will always be given what you need, not necessarily what you want.

The time has come for you to join with the Holy Spirit and manifest the best for all.

Time

Time keeps us rooted in the passage of death. We are born, we live, we die. Time is but a memory of a prison where we are not allowed to be ourselves. We are held captive to a passing idea that we are alone in a world full of people. Time dictates that we must be better than everyone else no matter the cost. The cost is great – the cost is ourselves.

We pass the time by ensuring that we are dutifully doing what we have been taught. We have been taught to be competitive, to struggle to obtain 'things' and to work at providing for our comfort. Our purpose is not known, other than to pass the time following the 'rules'. Whose rules? Where did time come from?

The answer to these questions comes from knowing our true selves. Time does not allow ourselves the luxury of getting to know oneself. We are so busy running around trying to satisfy all our human desires, wishes, dreams and ideas.

These are not important, what is important is to pass the time with the knowing of who you really are. You are the most important person in the world. What you think and how you think is what will release this world from time. It will release you from the cycle of time, where we are born, we live, we die.

Time is an invention, an elaborate scheme to keep us rooted in plainness. To show us that we are nothing but a puppet doing ego's bidding. The scene is scripted, the play's outcome sure.

Time passes and we continue to circle around, repeating the same patterns until we no longer know who we are. We are buried deep into a false belief that time is the only thing that matters. It does not!

Time is merely an end to a means. The means being a reminder of who we really are. We are love. Time can slow the process to the remembrance of this but can never stomp it out completely.

Time can only be encouraged to continue if you deny that you are love. Love is the total embodiment of the collapse of time. Time disappears when you accept your part in this play.

Accept you are love and let time slip away through your fingers, as it glistens through the passages of your renewed soul.

Time is but an everlasting memory where love has replaced time lost. Love has awakened the remembrance that time does not exist, only love does.

Change

Change is hard. It requires great strength to believe you can do it. To know you are leaving what is comfortable, even if it does not make you happy.

Changing the way you think is not without consequences. The dire consequences of not knowing brings fear to your every waking moment. You wonder what will happen and will you regret changing.

The sands of change will blow your way when you decide to make a change for the better. It may seem as if you made the wrong decision as you battle your way out of the deep tunnel of darkness you created. The winds will clear the path for you, so you may see clearly which way to go.

Following the light to a destination of change takes courage. The courage to know that what you are doing no longer makes sense to you. It no longer serves a purpose to remain as is.

Change requires you to be strong. Sure of yourself even if you are unsure of the outcome. You know with certainty the path to take.

Take the step into change and remember your courage. Remember you are doing this for yourself. You are changing for the better.

There may be bumps in the road and the winding road may seem as if you will never find the end. The end is near and the roadblocks in your path will be removed. The straight and narrow path has widened to give you room to grow.

Change requires dedicated determination. Although, at times, it will feel as though you have slipped backwards, do not despair. Pick yourself up, shake yourself off and try again.

No one learned how to walk without falling down. Keep trying and the change you want to happen will. If not in the time frame you wanted or in the way you wanted. Whatever change you choose will be for the best.

Trust yourself and change will happen. Always remember that there is a better way. A better way of helping yourself out of the deep dark recesses of a mind gone mad. Change releases you from the fear of retribution as you learn to accept love's way.

Patience

Patience is the promise of eternity. The eternity to know you are safe in love's embrace. It is a true knowing that no matter what happens, you will always be at peace.

Your peace is of utmost importance. By having peace, you are showing others how to be. The patience you show others when they are misguided indicates you are teaching love. You are helping them to follow love's guiding path.

Your patience can be tested at many times during your life. You may find yourself angry that no one is listening to you. You are trying to help a person to find a better way in life.

It is not up to you to know what is best for each person. What is up to you is to show patience by example. Your example shows that you are willing to live your light and to not compromise and fall down. You are willing to help uplift the emotional needs of persons known and unknown.

Only the Holy Spirit knows what is best for you. You may think you know what is best, but most of the time you are not thinking about the whole. You are only aware of a tiny small piece of the big picture.

By having patience, you are trusting that what happens is what is best for all. Being guided by the Holy Spirit, in a loving way, you are ensured you are on the path of remembrance.

Patience tells us by teaching patience - it is how we show kindness and compassion. The patience we show others is reflected back to ourselves, showing that we care. We care to grow into the loving being that we are.

Patience becomes the unending cycle of give and receive. We give patience, we receive patience. This cycle is the way to break the control we have over ourselves. The control that we believe we know what is best for ourselves. We do not!

Patience is the way home. Home to where all our sins are forgiven. To where we are love's embrace of light, kindness and compassion. Patience teaches us to be at peace with ourselves. When we are at peace with ourselves, we are at peace with others.

We know they are on their journey, just like we are. Our journeys may or may not intertwine, but we know we are helping the whole. Helping the pieces to fit back together so that the whole becomes one again.

Faith

Having faith is like believing a rock is going to walk. It is where you learn to trust yourself. It is part of the unseen and unknowing. Where you try to remember you are not alone.

Where does faith come from? From where the depths of your soul resides. From where truth begins and truth ends. It is a place where nothingness exists.

In the circle of life, faith intertwines the fabric of life. It is where you must learn to believe in yourself. That you are at the right moment, at the right time, in the right way.

There is nothing that can happen that does not happen exactly as it is supposed to. Faith tells us that believing in yourself creates a moment of stillness where all certainty resides. Certain that the sun will rise and time will cease to exist.

Where beauty resides, faith has restored to us the certainty of calmness. Of knowing that no matter what is happening, things are not always what they seem. It is a knowing, all is well.

The world fades, people shine, nature glows and your home is restored. It is where you learn to believe that you are guided to help restore faith to the lost ones. Where the lost ones return home to where all belongs. No one is lost, only misguided. Being misguided is not a sin. Only a step back from yourself and from faith. All can be returned to oneself.

Faith renews, restores and rejoins you to yourself and your most heavenly guidance. To be one with all who are holding the door open for you to step through.

Step through little one, into a most wonderous way of being. To the unseen world where colors are bright, sounds are clear, and smells remind you of your true home.

Where nothingness is everything and everything is all there is. It is a place that exists outside of time and space. Although hard to imagine, you know deep in your heart that is where you belong.

Only faith can bring you home. Home is where you belong.

Gratitude

Gratitude is the loving gift you give to yourself. Gratitude says you are on the verge of awakening to your true potential. It is a potential of abundance and kindness.

Sharing your store house of wealth with all you come in contact with. You begin to understand your true purpose here. The glowing embers of life itself begin to shine upon all.

Gratitude is the beginning of the end. Where you acknowledge you are ready to step into the bliss of being. Gratitude says we are all grateful for the opportunity to grow.

Growth begins with the shining example of one's true love. It towers within one's own heart. Warmth emanates from the sacred space of gratitude.

We are grateful for the opportunity to help others find their way. To be thankful for the honor to show them how to be. To truly understand it is our purpose to uplift others.

Our shining example creates a flow of grace and compassion. It is where we are humbled by the honor shown us. Our gratitude shows us the way home.

We begin the day by thanking the Holy Spirit for guiding us. We end the day by thanking the Holy

Spirit for guiding us. We are thankful for being in service to the Holy Spirit.

We are grateful we are one with the Holy Spirit. Their warm embrace and gentle loving guidance shine the way home. It gives us the courage to be fearless and humble.

It gives us the courage to know we are always helped and we are never alone. It gives us the knowledge we can release our fears and ego to the Holy Spirit, knowing we are always safe and protected.

Gratitude gives us the calmness to follow the loving way. The certainty to know we are on the right path. The ability to embrace showing others how to lift themselves from the depths of darkness.

We are the shining example of what love is. Being thankful gives us the chance to climb high above the clouds to look down upon a world gone mad. We are the light of the world.

Be grateful you are a soldier in this growing army of love. You are guiding all the disassociated souls to the light. You are showing them the way home.

Contentment

Contentment is peace resolved. When you no longer feel the need to be constantly looking for something new. When you no longer need validation from another person.

You are content when you are happy with who you are. You are happy with how your life is and you are happy with how things are going in your life.

Contentment is peace expressed in subtle ways. It is the smile you have while drinking your coffee in the morning. It is the serenity at enjoying a beautiful sunset. It is the enjoyment of a rainy day, sitting by the fire, enjoying just being.

Contentment comes when you no longer feel the need to judge others. You no longer need to compare yourself to others. You no longer need to worry about what others think of you.

You walk the walk and talk the talk of someone sure of themselves. Sure in the sense of knowing you are well taken care of. Knowing you no longer need to hunt for more.

You have arrived at peace. You have learned to release all stress in your life. You know with certainty that all will be as it is supposed to be.

You understand you are not in control. You let go of the requirement that you direct yourself and others. You now know your higher guidance knows what is best for you.

You are content to follow your loving guidance knowing it will be what is best for all. You walk the path of shining light where each step you take releases a fragrant scent. You are healing yourself and others.

Your contentment comes at no cost. It comes with open arms waiting to embrace you with light and love. To wrap you in angel songs, lifting you up to heaven. Contentment is heaven on earth.

Happiness

Happiness is the road to recovery. Laughter makes you feel good. Smiling lets you know you are happy.

Happiness does not come from outside of you. It comes from within the deep recesses of your soul. It is a deep-seated thought brought to the forefront to be expressed outward.

Happiness is contagious. If you feel happy, others around you feel happy. Misery has been left in the dust. Blown away and shattered to the winds of change.

Only you can make yourself happy. No one else is responsible for your happiness. Only you are.

Learn to smile at the smallest accomplishment. Learn to laugh at the gentlest of jokes. Learn to be happy with yourself.

Start small and let happiness seep into all your pores. As you begin to fill up with happiness, your bucket will overflow. The overflow spreads to a world unhappy.

The sad eyes and down turned lips begin to change. Shoulders are pushed back and backs are straight. You walk with purpose spreading your wings for all to see.

You are blessed to share your happiness. Your joy shows through. Nothing can diminish your joy at knowing you are home.

You want others to join you in your happiness. Let them come and learn how to be joyous. Let them begin to open to their own happiness.

Not all are ready to be happy. Show them they deserve to be happy. Show them they are worthy of joy. Show them it is their right to be happy.

Everyone who touches your happiness will start to imagine that maybe they can be happy. Let the seeds planted grow in their own time. The seeds of love grow into a beautiful blossoming you.

Hope

Hope is the desire for an expected outcome. Hope is the belief you will get what you want. Hope is the wish for something better.

Unsupported hope is never satisfied. There is always the need to get something, regardless if it is helpful or not. It is your desire that drives hope.

Is your hope for the best? Do you wish the best for yourself and everyone? Does hope satisfy your request for something?

Only when you join with the Holy Spirit is hope satisfied. Hope is now supported, supported by your higher guidance. You think you know what it is you hope for, but only the Holy Spirit knows what it is you really hope for.

What you really hope for is peace and happiness. Regardless of what you think you hope for, once you have peace and happiness, hope is fulfilled.

Hope springs forth and flows in tune with your highest desire. You begin to realize you have been lost among the stars wandering from place to place.

Where is home? As you let hope become a part of you, you begin to see the light. You are drawing closer to where you belong. You belong where hope is forever satisfied.

Reaching for the stars and coming up empty is not the way. You come up empty when you believe wandering around is the only way to live. Learn to live with a hopeful purpose. A purpose where you are shown how to hope.

Hope is the way of the enlightened ones. They know, with certainty, they are on the path of inner peace. With inner peace comes a knowing, hope will always be cared for.

Love

Love is something we all profess to know what it is. We speak the words and feel we know what it is. We dream dreams of love where the perfect mate comes into our lives and showers us with their loving thoughts, ideas and embrace.

We know this person loves us because of all the flowering praise they give us and how they bow at every step we take and every word we speak. We profess to know love by how each person in our life sings our praise and ensures our continued success by helping us in all our endeavors.

This is not love! Love is a feeling and unspoken kindness, a warm embrace, an awareness that love is all around us. Love is a smile in security of knowing we are all taken care of. Love is a quiet moment of reflection where we know, with certainty, that all is right and good.

Love is knowing there is no conflict, that no matter what challenges you are faced with, the outcome will always be what is best for all. What is best for all is the knowing that no matter what appears to be happening, if allowed, love will always guide your thoughts and actions.

What is love? Love is the security of being one's self with no fear of retribution from another. Love is choosing the path that leads to oneness, where oneness is the surprise of certainty, of happiness, no matter what is happening.

Love is a feeling, a knowingness of calmness where strings are straight and untangled. The path is wide and open, waiting for you to walk it.

Once on the path there is no turning back. Love guides us to an end of the beginning, where a single touch awakens the flower of our hearts. Just be in the moment, where love resides and become love's embrace.

Forgiveness

Forgiveness is the way. What does this mean? It means that you are ready to release the past and not worry about the future. It means you accept your innocence and want to help others find their innocence.

By innocence, we mean that you have learned to let go of yourself and release yourself to the Holy Spirit. It is an understanding where you acknowledge no one has done anything wrong. It is where you truly understand you are meant to help others to find themselves. By helping others to find themselves, you find yourself.

We only find ourselves when we teach love. Love by example is harder than you think. You encompass the embodiment of now. Now is the moment of stillness where all is known. When all is known, then love is.

Love is the reflection of your beauty within. To live by love and to teach love, kindness must be shown. When kindness is shown, then love has arrived.

Sharing kindness to all is easier said than done. Kindness must be shown to even your perceived 'enemy'. To all who have angered or annoyed you.

For love to shine, kindness must be ingrained into your soul.

When you step back from kindness, then forgive yourself. Forgiving yourself shows that you are aware of your commitment to love. Love heals all and forgiveness is the way.

Thoughts

You think it, you own it. Thoughts always come first, before words and actions. Do not think because they are your thoughts that they are hidden from the outside world. Nothing could be further from the truth.

Your inside world and outside world are the same. You think if you keep your thoughts to yourself you are protected from harm. You cause yourself great harm when you think unsavory thoughts. Any thought that does not wish the best for someone gives you pain.

The pain may show up in your physical body. It may show up in your emotions. It may show up in your interactions with other people. It will always cause you harm in untold ways.

Thoughts are everything. They determine how you see the world. Do you see suffering? Do you see goodness? Do you see the best in people? Do you see the worst in people?

Your thoughts determine how peaceful you want to be. Do you want to know that helping others gives you peace? Follow your loving guidance to know the best way you can help.

Be vigilant with your thoughts. Judgements, of any kind, cause you to step back. You must be sure your thoughts are of the most compassionate to move forward.

Thoughts of kindness grow. Thoughts of hatred diminish the growth of kindness. Your thoughts are who you are. Take care of your thoughts and they will take care of you.

Do not despair. As you are learning to release your unkind thoughts, you will feel like you are moving backwards. Your storehouse of kindness will grow beyond your kept thoughts of fear. Whenever you are not sure of yourself, ask to be reminded of all the kindnesses you have accomplished.

Thoughts always come first. This is where you learn to correct yourself. Where you learn to become a loving person filled with compassion. Compassion for understanding each of us is on their own journey.

Their journeys interact with you. You are here to help each other remember home. You only remember home by monitoring your thoughts. When you step back from pure thoughts, forgive yourself. It takes a lot of practice to do this, i.e., a lot of forgiveness.

Is it worth it? Oh my, yes! The work you put in is the work you get out. Clean thoughts make you feel better. Thoughts of love and the thought of sharing the love, helps you remember the way home.

Inspiration

Have you ever wondered where your inspiration or ideas come from? The loving inspiration comes from up above. The fear-based ideas come from down below.

Inspiration is the free-flowing exchange of ideas. Ideas which are for the betterment of mankind. An inspiration can be as small as – should I have a cup of coffee this morning?

The size of the inspiration does not matter. What does matter is that the inspiration is loving. The outcome will always be what is best for yourself and for all.

Inspiration is the joining of minds. While there is only one mind, you are rejoining yourself to the one true guide. The only guide that wants what is best for you.

Once you rejoin yourself to the loving guidance you so richly deserve, you find your life flows more smoothly. The babbling brook slowly meanders along, happy in the knowing that sharing your inspiration is opening you to untold wonders.

You realize you have been buried deep within a crumbling tower. Hidden from sight, protected by a false sense of kingliness. Your inspirations have been turned off and you have listlessly wandered.

Time for your hapless wandering to stop. Time for you to believe your ideas have merit. Time to trust your loving guidance.

As you become more comfortable with joining with your higher guidance, you become surer of yourself. Your inspiration does not need to be big, grandiose ideas. Just ideas that help humanity.

A kind word, a loving hug, a hearty laugh are all inspirations. Listening to a person in need, a smile, a sharing of ideas is how you begin to become comfortable in learning to be one.

True inspiration is when you are joined with yourself and your higher guidance. Inspiration will happen when you are ready to accept your role in the upliftment of humanity. When you are ready to open yourself to the light within.

Healing

When does healing happen? When you change your mind. You change your mind to be guided by the Holy Spirit. You choose not to be ruled by the ego.

It has been eons of you following ego's restrictive ways. It is time to choose a new way of thinking. It may be strange to you at first, but worth it in the end.

As you begin to heal from thoughts of despair, hopelessness and unworthiness, you may feel lost. You are not sure if this is the right path to follow. You have so long been comfortable with what you think is how things should be.

You believe you are here to suffer. Suffering comes in many forms. You see others suffer and wonder; do you deserve better?

Yes, you do. You can heal and, in your healing, others are helped. You wonder how is this possible? Will you feel guilty at being healed and happy when so many are suffering? Shouldn't you be like them and follow the crowd. Be one with the miserable.

No! How are the downtrodden to learn how to pull themselves out of darkness unless you show them. Your happiness gives hope that it is possible to spring forth open to what you deserve.

Healing is about joining with the Holy Spirit and being guided to heal your mind. Healing happens in the mind. When the mind is healed, you are able to teach others how to heal.

Healing brings untold fortunes of golden rays of happiness. It shines away the recesses of darkness hidden in a mind filled with fear and insanity. The fear and insanity diminish into nothingness, leaving you with a feeling of supreme calmness.

A calmness that emanates out of all of you. Everyone feels the calmness and it begins to have them question - "how do I get this feeling all the time?"

You show them how to join with the Holy Spirit. Knowing as each one learns to join together, a healing happens. Healing is of the mind and that is where you learn to change. Learn to love all.

Acceptance

When you accept something, you often feel like you have given something up. You feel like you have resigned yourself to feeling out of control. You feel like you lost.

Sometimes with acceptance you feel you have to give up your individuality. Know this - there is no individuality. We are all one, joined minds, sharing thoughts and ideas.

Accepting this is hard. The ego will do whatever it has to, to remind you that you are an individual. You are separate from each other and your one true home.

By living this way, you have accepted littleness. When you feel you have to give up something to get something, you are in a win-lose situations. If you feel you have to resign yourself to whatever, you have given up. If you feel like you lost, you accepted resentment and anger.

These traits are not becoming to one who has it all. Not all, in the sense of worldly possessions, but all in the sense you are becoming rich with peace and happiness. Knowing these are your birthright, you now need to claim them.

Accept you are important and you matter. Go forth and share your acceptance with all you touch.

Light the way in a path of darkness. Let the light bulb snap on and accept your greatness.

There are legions of souls waiting to welcome you back into the fold of love. They are gently guiding you to accept your place amongst them. You have been greatly missed.

Truth

What is truth? The truth is you do not know who you are. You believe you are a body you inhabit. You believe that you are restricted to this tiny, small, insignificant body.

You believe the body protects you. You are constantly fussing over the body. You believe the body shows the world who you are. You believe the body is the most important thing there is.

The truth is you are not a body. You are here, in a body, because you chose to believe you know best. You chose to join with the ego and explore what it is like to suffer. You suffer a fool's delight in the sacrifices you made to be here in a body.

Your affinity for the body is well known. You secretly like it when you see someone else suffer. It makes you feel better about yourself. You think, they have it worse than you, so you are better off than they are.

Truth would never want to see someone or something else suffer. Your ego-self tells you; you are justified in relishing the suffering of another. Yet, truth would ask you to help the sufferer.

Remember truth is not a body. Truth is the all-encompassing belief we are all one. Bodies are not one but minds join as one.

Truth reminds us we are more than a body. We are our mind. A mind that exists outside of time and space. While we are here, we have the ability to connect to the mind. The ability to connect to the love that the mind is.

We remember the truth of ourselves. We remember truth is the way home. Truth is the only way to live. Truth brings us to the love we so desperately want and need.

Universal Love

The innocence of a child is the ultimate of Universal Love. A child knows no boundaries and is open to sharing their feelings and observations. A child simply decides what it needs or wants and obtains it. A child knows no limitations. They are free to be themselves without others imparting to them their boundaries, limits and issues.

It is in the innocence where Universal Love lies. The innocence of wonder, amazement and the newness of all that exists.

Universal Love has no boundaries, no limitations, it just is. It is a love that surrounds and permeates all that exists. It radiates an essence of supreme kindness. It sparkles like the stars up above and shines so brightly that is fills all that is.

Universal Love is a way of life. It is where one becomes the innocence of the child. Where they see, know, and feel the enjoyment in whatever they are doing. Where one gives of themselves freely to their own loving essence. When one gives freely to their own loving essence, they are opening themselves up to limitless possibilities.

Life is not meant to be hard. It is meant to be enjoyed and shared. One can only find their bliss and joy by experiencing life in this earthly world.

Try new things, meet new people, go new places. Get out and open new doorways for yourself. Find what brings you the most joy by being joy itself.

Open to Universal Love and become yourself.

Abundance

Abundance is not about material possessions. It is not about collecting more things. Abundance is not about having more than another.

Abundance is being thankful for what you do have. It is about expressing gratitude for the small things as well as the large things. It is about sharing what you have with others.

You give abundance away to get abundance. You have no fear - you will be taken care of. The abundance you give away will be returned to you.

This does not mean giving all your possessions away, unless you are guided to do so. It does mean you learn to give kindness, compassion and smiles. These things you have in abundance and it costs nothing to give away.

You are not sacrificing anything by giving what you already have in excess. You have an excess of happiness you want to share with others. What you give, you receive back.

As you walk in a field of flowers, the flowers crane their necks to absorb your abundance. You emanate love and compassion which helps others to heal and grow. The abundance you give others spreads outwards.

You are grateful for the opportunity to share your abundance. You are grateful to acknowledge that abundance is more than material possessions. It is about what is available for all.

All have the right to live a life of peace and full of abundance. Abundance which gives all the opportunity to share in the wealth of love.

God's Love

You are a child of God. God only has eyes for you. He sees a perfect child. A child that remembers his love.

Remembering God's love is the most beautiful, wonderous and peaceful thing in this world. The warm glow that covers you in the golden rays of love. Wrapping you in a warm fleece giving you a cozy, peaceful feeling.

God's love is like a butterfly flittering from flower to flower, drinking the sweet nectar. The sweet nectar sustains the butterfly to bloom into beautiful colors. The colors of the rainbow meld together to create a kaleidoscope of wonderous sights.

God's love sustains you and lets you become the loving; kind child God knows you to be. You are the apple in God's eye. The shining star of the perfect child who honors God's love.

When you honor God's love, you are honoring yourself. You believe you are worthy of God's love. God's warm embrace lets you know you are not forgotten.

You are always in God's mind and thoughts. God always wants you to be safe and protected.

God desires for you what God desires for God's self.

The love God has for you, once realized, brings tears to your eyes. You wondered why you stayed away so long. You wondered why you ever left God's all-encompassing belief in you.

God believes in you so much that God does not know the broken, lost child. God only knows you have returned. Happy in the knowing you are safe.

God's only desire for you is for you to be at peace with yourself. For you to know you are forever welcomed home. All perceived sins are forgiven, never to be recognized. God knows you are home because he feels complete you are there.

You feel complete you have joined with God's love. You are whole and ready to take your place beside God. You are ready to help others to remember God's love.

Section 4 – Meditations

Open Your Heart

Sit comfortably in a chair with your arms resting softly in your lap, both feet are flat on the ground and your back is straight.

Close your eyes. Take three long, slow, deep breaths. Relax deeper and deeper after each breath. Let all thoughts drift away into nothingness. Rest in the knowing that no harm can come to you.

Imagine a brilliant white light emanating from your heart center. The white light slowly envelops you until there is nothing to see but white light. You feel warm, safe and joyous. A smile comes to you.

You find yourself feeling light and airy. You begin to feel yourself lift off the chair. You are light as a feather. Any denseness and darkness have been melted away by the white light.

Then, you find yourself encircled by thin golden threads. The threads form a geometric pattern around you. Each thread pulsates with golden light. The white light becomes brighter and more brilliant. It is a white unknown here.

The golden threads begin to fade as the geometric pattern gets absorbed into your energy fields. You feel alive and energized. You have never felt more awake than you do now.

Slowly you begin to float back to the chair you are sitting in. You feel a sense of calmness that you have never felt before. A sense of supreme peace. You know with certainty; all is well.

Take a slow, long, deep breath. Take another slow, long, deep breath. Slowly open your eyes. Readjust yourself to your surroundings. Sit quietly in the chair until you feel you are fully aware of your surroundings.

As you open your heart, rest in the knowing that you are safe and all is well.

Remembering Home

Sit comfortably in a chair with your arms resting softly in your lap, both feet are flat on the ground and your back is straight.

Take three long, slow, deep breaths. Relax your body by letting all thoughts of concern drain away from you.

Imagine you are surrounded by a golden white light. This golden white light permeates your body. All parts of you are now a golden white light.

Imagine at your heart center a flower bud. The bud is tightly closed. Slowly one petal of the flower opens. As it opens, a small puff of air is released.

You notice another petal is slowly opening. It also releases a puff of air. As each petal opens, a wave of air is created by the opening petals, encompasses you in peace.

The ruffled edges of each petal remind you of a soft warm feeling of long ago. The ruffled edges gently sway back and forth. On each sway, you see a flicker of light.

The swaying becomes faster and faster. The flicker of light becomes more. The light is an open doorway to the inner recesses of your hidden soul.

The doorway is open for you to walk through. Walk through to the remembrance of a long-ago place, where you know with all certainty, you are home.

Enjoy being home. Remember the joy and happiness you feel at being joined with all. Rest in the knowing you will return.

Slowly take three long, deep breaths bringing you back to your temporary home. You smile knowing you can visit at any time.

Slowly open your eyes and see how things look different. Notice how you feel different. Know that things will not ever be the same.

You remember home with each deep breath and the feeling of serenity.

Meet Your Guides

Sit comfortably in a chair with your arms resting softly in your lap, both feet are flat on the ground and your back is straight.

Close your eyes and take a slow deep breath. Release the breath slowly and relax your shoulders. Let the stress of your day fall away.

Take another slow deep breath. As you release the breath, imagine a golden light around you. The light fills you with peace and serenity.

Take another slow deep breath. Release this breath slowly. As you release this breath, you find yourself standing by a bubbling stream with dappled light flickering on the water.

You stand there for a few moments and you enjoy the beautiful warm breeze on your face. The sounds of birds singing and of bees buzzing. The river flowers release a slight fragrant scent which wafts its way to you. You find yourself emersed in the beauty of it all.

Slowly, you notice someone walking towards you. They are dressed in a white flowing gown and have a radiant glow about them. They seem calm and loving.

You feel safe knowing that they are here to help you. The person bows to you and then introduces themself. This person suggests that you both walk along the stream for a while. As you walk along the stream, the path moves away from the stream.

You find yourself walking along a wooded path. You notice that the path is slowly climbing up a gentle hill. At the top of the gentle hill, there is a beautiful open meadow.

In the middle of the meadow is a chair. The chair is decorated with jewels that sparkle like the stars up above. The chair has an ember-like glow about it. It has a flowing see-through appearance to it. It shimmers with radiant light.

The person you are with beckons you to sit in the chair. You gently lower yourself into the chair to find the chair is light as a feather and very comfortable. The person who brought you there, steps back from you.

As you relax in the chair, suddenly, you are encircled by 12 people dressed in the same white flowing gowns. All 12 people bow to you in unison. You find yourself mesmerized by the beauty, serenity and peacefulness that emanates from each person.

Slowly one of the persons walks forward to you. They lay a gift at your feet and then impart a pearl of wisdom to you. As each person moves forward and presents their gift and wisdom, you find yourself full of gratitude at the humbleness you are feeling.

When all 12 are done, they reform the circle and gently sing an angelic song to you. The music reverberates through you. The gentle swaying of harmony fills you with peace and serenity. You are honored to be there.

As the singing slowly finishes, each person bows to you, one at a time, whereby creating a wave of light that encircles you. Then, all 12 bow to you at the same time. You bow back to them; grateful you have been part of this ceremony.

All 12 people have left and the person who brought you to this place of gathering has appeared at your side. It is time to meander back through the forest path. To walk along the stream to where you met the person who guided you on this journey. You bow to each other knowing you will meet again.

Slowly take a deep breath
Rest in the knowing you are safe
Slowly take another deep breath
Believe in yourself that love's light is part of you
Slowly take another deep breath

When you are ready, blink your eyes open. Take a few moments to readjust yourself to the room you are in. Look around and notice what you see.

Take another deep breath and know that you are loved by all.

Section 5 – Reflections

Your Choice

There is a broken down, decrepit house up on a hill. As you walk the path, up the hill, the trees are all dead and withered. There is no sound of birds singing, or the wind blowing, or rustling of the leaves. There is no color of flowers – everything looks dark and burnt.

As you near the house, the door opens. Inside is the most beautiful, warm golden light you have ever seen. You stand at the threshold of the open door and you are deciding – do you stay in the broken-down dark world that you have become accustomed to or do you walk over the threshold and through the open doorway into the warm and beautiful golden light?

The door has been opened for you. Only you can walk through it.

As you walk the path of light you will meet many people or situations that will show you the way. They will point the way and open the doors to opportunity.

Will you see the opening and walk the path towards greater love?

Will you step into the light of love and become the golden ray of yourself?

Are you committed to yourself?

Are you ready to love yourself?

Pure love does not have any conditions. Love is not blind but fear is.

Nature

In the beauty of nature, you find a grain of truth. The grain is but a small remembrance of where you come from. Nature reminds us that give and take are a fragile balance. The balancing act of too much and too little.

It is where we see the blossoming of one's own heart. The dew drops of truth as seen through the clearness of water. The sun shining bright reminding us of the natural glow of our own essence.

Nature also shows us the dry and withering sands where the roots of life are dying. The birds are dropping like flies and the cracked earth swallows them up never to be seen again. It is where the clouds cover the sun but no rain comes to nourish the Earth. The thickness of the air chokes us where we are unable to renew ourselves. The withering plants scream for water but none comes.

Nature tells us how we are doing. It is a reflection of the health of ourselves. As nature lives, we live. As nature dies, we die.

Long ago in a time where man did not exist, nature owned the earth. Nature wandered the Earth blessing all that was touched. The abundance of nature was shared with all.

There was no sense of lack. Only the pleasure of knowing all is well. The well spring of life's fountain rises high above the clouds. Letting the sun shine forth to renew nature.

All of nature is intertwined with itself. Give and take constantly needing to be balanced. It is at the center point where balance is found. Too little, too much, just right is all found in nature.

Nature reminds us of the beauty within. Where we learn the truth about ourselves. It is where time stands still and the ripples of life renew us.

Nature knows us. It knows we need the connection of oneness to survive the balancing act of too little or too much. It is where we come to know all is well.

Nature's bounty reminds us of the coming storm. The storm where we choose –

Do we live in love? or

Do we live in fear?

Destination

As we fly to our destination, we float through the clouds, the gentle breeze on our face, the warmth of the sun on our skin and the dew drops sparkle on our eyelashes.

We know we are safe high above the clouds looking down upon a world full of life. The life of our souls blends together to bring joy to all. We are one with the Earth and all who inhabit her. She is our safe haven.

The lush green fields, the clear blue waters, the majestic mountains, and the bright yellow sun is the beauty we see. The colorful rainbows, the birds singing, the flowers blooming and the sparkle of the jewels in each one's eyes as they marvel at the beauty to behold.

We join with all to share the ever-expanding bounty of love. A love that has no boundaries and is not limited by time, space or distance.

This love is the love of your soul, to be shared with whomever you touch with your gentle eyes, softly spoken word, and your magical touch. A touch that sends shivers down the spine and lights up all that there is of each other. We share your ever-expanding awareness of loves blossom.

As we fly to our destination, we float through the clouds, the gentle breeze on our face, the warmth of the sun on our skin, the dew drops on our eyelashes ever refreshing us. Reminding us that we are the bright star that lights the way home for all our souls.

A Peaceful Way

A Peaceful Way was written for a person who had recently lost their husband.

I sent them one line of the saying per week. They were to read the line as many times per day as they could remember. At the very least, they were to repeat the line, morning, noon and night.

The following week I would send another line of the saying. Again, they were to repeat that line as many times as possible each day.

This continued for nine weeks. One week for each line of the saying. At the end of the nine weeks, I sent them the saying all put together.

The person I wrote this for did tell me that they found it to be very helpful and it helped them to release their grief. They, of course, still remember and miss their husband, but it is not as painful for them as it was in the beginning.

On the next page is A Peaceful Way for you to read. Please follow your guidance as to whether you read it all the way through or you read one line per week, then read it all put together.

A Peaceful Way

My journey is not over

Help is on the way

Trials and tribulations are one

My guide walks with me

Stop – look around

Beauty is everywhere

I am the light of the world

Tears of joy spring forth

I am well

A Prayer for Oneself and Humanity

For everyone on the planet to see their light within, to feel the love of themselves, and to know their beauty.

To grow beyond their wildest imagination and to know joy and peace and love is theirs to behold.

For the light to shine upon them as they grow brighter and brighter.

For their essence to be filled with wonder and awe at all the support and love they have.

For their spirit to truly know their soul.

To become one with the highest vibration so they join the legions of souls who are growing and expanding into the all-knowing.

For each and every individual to meld into the sea of possibilities and choose what is best for them.

To explore their limitless imagination and to share their boundless joy with the world.

For all to come to know they are the light and the love they all seek.

To no longer need to seek outside themselves for knowledge, direction and guidance.

For all to know they are loving beacons of light that are upon the threshold of a new beginning. A beginning that will show all a new way of being.

Conclusion

Did you know human beings are only capable of two emotions: love or fear. Fear has many names such as anger, hate, despair, guilt, worry, pain, doubt, etc. Love only has one.

After reading *Love Awakens You*, you are now more aware of the differences between love and fear. You have learned to open yourself to love, whereby diminishing fear. The benefits you feel are loss of loneliness, more self-confidence, greater serenity and the ability to choose love over fear.

There is a growing number of people who are opening up to love. As more and more people expand their awareness of love, increases in love and light are shining throughout the Earth. You have joined with people who are helping with the upliftment of humanity. Not only are you helping others, you are helping yourself become the best version of you.

May your journey be filled with love and light
May your light become a shining beacon
May your beautiful soul blossom
May you always choose love

In love and light,

Cindi Buckley

Acknowledgements

As a student of *A Course in Miracles*, I would be remiss in not thanking the Holy Spirit for helping me, guiding me, teaching me and correcting me. They are always, lovingly, reminding me of who I really am. Their unending support and love have allowed me to write this book.

Thank you to my husband, "the grammar police", for correcting all my grammar, punctuation and spelling (of which there was plenty!). Even if he was not allowed to change the wording (which was hard for him!). His support and guidance have been invaluable.

Thank you to my dear friend, Judy Samloff, for giving me Gary R. Renard's *The Disappearance of the Universe* book which started this journey I am now on. Judy was also one of the first people to read the book. Her advice made for a better book.

Thank you to Elissa Heyman, the psychic in Santa Fe, who gave me my first crystal. A beautiful citrine point which I still have 22 years later.

Thank you to Catherine Eisley, my Spiritual Awareness instructor, who told me I would be writing inspiration sayings. I, of course, did not believe her at the time.

Thank you to Brett Hilker, my coach at Self-Publishing School, for the book's subtitle and much needed advice on wording for the back cover. Luckily, he is in tune with his inspiration.